For Atticus, Scout, and especially Athen,
who didn't pray until he did.

I PRAY, YOU PRAY

BY
RILEY TAYLOR

ILLUSTRATED BY
Аня Барченко

I pray, you pray

She prays, he prays

We pray, they pray

We pray in Jesus' name.

I know that when I pray to God,
I'm talking to my Father;
He hears and knows and loves to answer
All his sons and daughters!

Every day I pray with hope
And ask him for his kingdom,
To rule my heart and help my friends
And give me kingly wisdom.

When all the world seems scary
And I just want to scream
I scream my fears in prayer to him
'Cause God is on my team!

"Would you pray for me?"

"I'd love to pray for you!"

When I think of naughty things
To say or think or do
I pray, "God, lead me far from there
And back to loving you!"

When I sin (I know I do)
It hurts my Father's heart;
I pray "I'm sorry! Please forgive me,
I need a brand new start."

When friends do things that hurt me
Help me forgive them too,
The same way you've forgiven me
And told me, "I love you."

For all the things I need each day,
God says ask and knock and find
There are many things that I can pray
And God hears every time!

Let's take a big

HUGE

                                            breath

And let it out

                  reallll slowwww . . .

Then pray,

"Thank you for my life,
And for helping me to grow!"

THANK YOU

FATHER

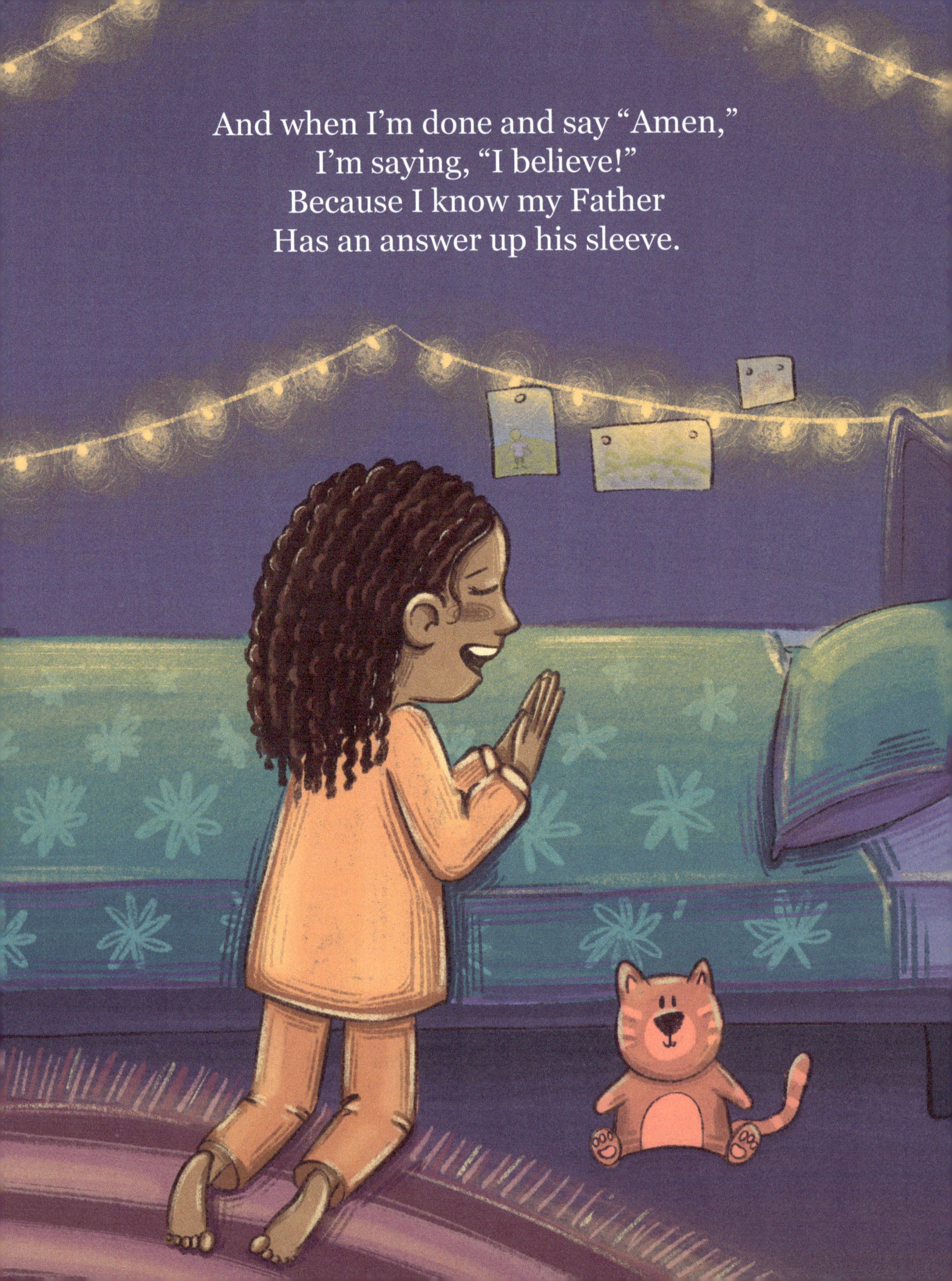

Let's pray for those we care about
God loves them all the same.
Aunts and uncles, friends and cousins
Can we think of more by name?

Let's pray now to our Father!

"Dear God . . .

        Thank you . . .

        I'm feeling . . .

        I'm sorry . . .

        Please . . ."

I pray, you pray

She prays, he prays

We pray, they pray

We pray in Jesus' name...

Amen!

ABOUT THE AUTHOR

Riley Taylor is an Elder and the director of preaching and vision at Calvary Fellowship in Mountlake Terrace, Washington—a large, growing church located in the suburbs of Seattle.

A musician and filmmaker, Riley's work has been seen on Netflix and Amazon Prime, as well as on TBN. He holds a Masters in Applied Biblical Leadership from Western Seminary in Portland, Oregon.

Riley is married to Bhritney, and they have three kids: Atticus, Scout, and Athen.

RILEYDTAYLOR.COM

ABOUT THE ILLUSTRATOR

Currently residing in Uzhgorod, a city in western Ukraine, Аня Барченко ("Anya") was born in the East but had to move with family due to the war. She has loved to draw since childhood, and with support from family and friends, has been studying graphic design for three years. Anya views illustration as a way to express her heart and soul, share ideas, and evoke emotion in every person who enjoys her art.

INSTAGRAM.COM/BARCHENKOANNA

Copyright © 2022 Riley Taylor

All rights reserved. No part of this book may be reproduced or used in any manner without the prior written permission of the copyright owner, except for the use of brief quotations in a book review.

To request permissions, contact the publisher at rileydtaylor@gmail.com.

Hardcover: 979-8-218-09908-4
Paperback: 979-8-218-09909-1

First paperback edition November 2022.

Edited by Peter Baumgartner
Illustrations by Аня Барченко
Layout by Riley Taylor

Printed by Ingram Spark in the USA.

Riley Taylor
PO Box 128
Mountlake Terrace, WA 98043

rileydtaylor@gmail.com